Our beautiful hair is a work of art.

When it comes to our hair, we follow our heart.

Look but don't touch our beautiful hair.

Depending on our mood is the style we'll wear.

Our beautiful hair is our visible crown.

Our hair makes a statement without a sound.

Our hair sets all kinds of beautiful trends.

How we wear our hair it all depends.

Curls and puffs or braids and beads,

Lets celebrate our hair-story from Miss Dejha B!

Kids Hair Story

© 2022 by Dejha B. All rights reserved.

First Published in the United States of America in 2022
by Black Angel Publishing.

First Printing, 2022

No part of this book may be reproduced in any manner whatsoever
without written permission of the author, Dejha B, Dejha B Coloring LLC or the publisher,
Black Angel Publishing except for use of brief quotations in a book review.

ISBN-978-1-7359976-8-1

Created and Conceptualized by Dejha B

Illustrations by: Dejha B

For More Coloring Books Visit:

www.dejhabcoloring.com

THIS HAIRSTORY BELONGS TO

In the early 1970s, wearing an Afro represented the Black is beautiful movement!

I love wearing my Afro-Puffs. It makes me feel naturally beautiful!

I love my hair!

Activity:

Write down all the things you love about your hair.

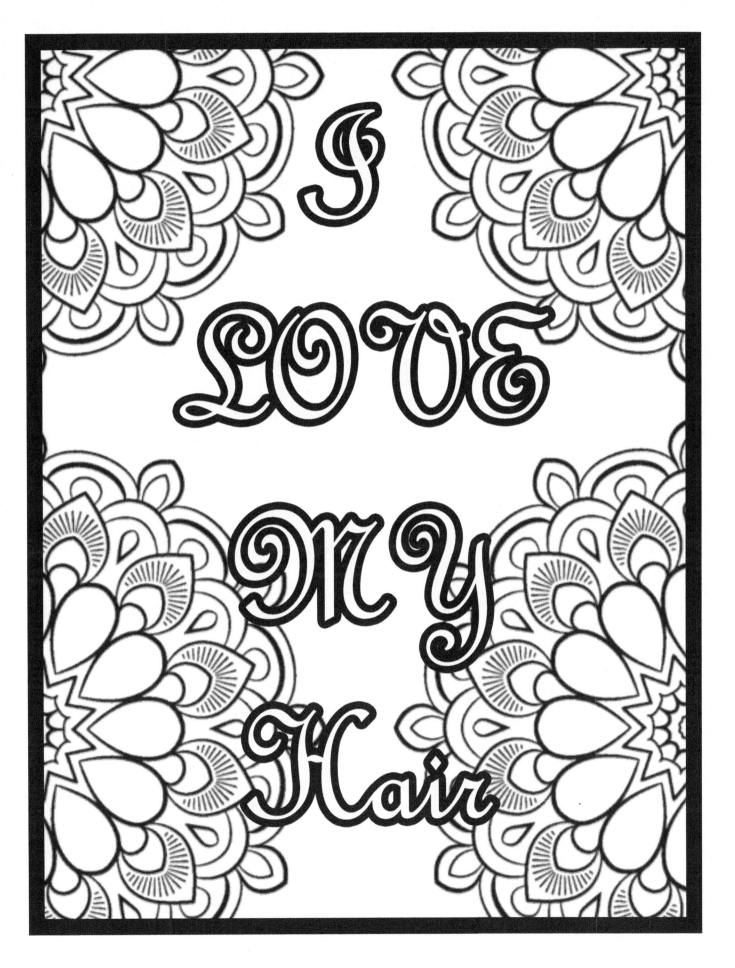

My ponytails brings out my beautiful eyes!

I make my braid into a visible crown to show I am a princess!

I'm camera ready!

My big hair matches my big personality!

I wear my braids and beads as a symbol to remind me of my ancestors strength throughout history.

I express my creativity with my hair!

I love my natural hair!

In the 1920s, also known as the roaring twenties, many women wore their hair in soft wavy hairstyles.

When It's picture day, my mom curls my hair!

I love my natural bang.

Crochet braids is a method of hooking synthetic hair extensions to a person's natural hair.

I love my afro!

I love my Mohawk. It brings out my inner Afro-Punk! Originating with warriors of Native American tribes, the name "Mohawk" comes from the indigenous people of the Mohawk nation.

I have a fresh new silk press!

A silk press is the process of straightening natural hair without using a relaxer. Annie Malone was the first to patent the hot comb in the 1900s.

Bantu Knots, sometimes referred to as Nubian Knots, have been around for over 100 years, and still are popular today. "Bantu" is a term that describes the various ethnic groups within Southern Africa that spoke the Bantu language. In recent years women have worn it as a protective style or a way to achieve a defined curly style when taken out.

I love wearing my baby hairs out and laying my edges. Wearing your baby hairs are the short hairs around the hairline and can be a work of art. It can be traced to the roaring 1920s when civil right activist and singer Josephine Baker made it popular amongst African American women.

Can you name some more celebrities that made it popular in the 80s, 90s or in recent times?

Find the following hairstyles in the word search.

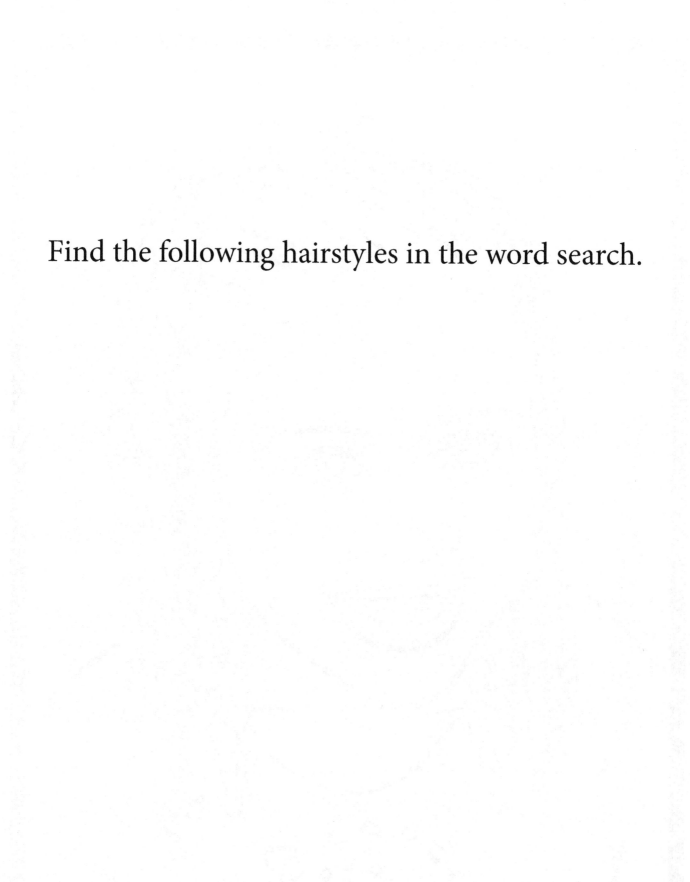

Word Search

```
S C J J F J B B F E P N N W I G S D
P O H Y B N E A I F I L U I J E G V
I R O M O A A N N R G O B I F L S A
N N I C X F D G G E T C I N T Q B Z
C R K U B R S S E N A K A B W P O J
U O I R R O Q S R C I S N R I A B A
R W K L A P C I W H L K K A S X B F
L S L S I U V L A R S C N I T M U R
S Q H C D F H U V O X Q O D H C N O
T I F R S F T N E L M N T S O T S X
A O D X J S B L S L E R S E W O L I
A K P O N Y T A I L Q W A V E S U E
```

Find the following words in the puzzle.
Words are hidden → ↓ and ↘ .

AFRO
AFRO PUFFS
BANGS
BEADS
BOB
BOX BRAIDS
BRAIDS

BUNS
CORNROWS
CURLS
FINGER WAVES
FRENCH ROLL
LOCKS
NUBIAN KNOTS

PIGTAILS
PIN CURLS
PONYTAIL
TWIST
WAVES
WIGS

The first known examples of dreadlocks date back to ancient Egyptians. Dreadlocks have become popular and people wear this hairstyle for many reasons. Some reasons are religious, fashion, cultural pride, or spiritual beliefs.

My hairstyle makes me feel like a star!

My hair is beautiful!

MY HAIR

IS BEAUTIFUL

When I want to play with my friends, I wear my two jumbo braids!

How often do you change your hairstyle?

I Change My Hair Often!

My naturally defined curls look amazing on me!

Cornrows have been around for centuries in African culture. In many African cultures, different styles and patterns of cornrows were a way to identify which tribe you belonged to. Your braided style could give an indication of your martial status, age, wealth, and religion. In America, the slaves called it cornrows because it reminded them of the cornfields.

I love my new hairstyle with my pretty braids and bows!

I love my Fulani braids!
Fulani braids are popular with the Fulani people of Africa. It has become popular with many celebrities on the red carpet. Some key elements of the Fulani hairstyle is conrows stretching from the front to the back. The hairstyle also features two braids on the side with beads or accessories, and finished off with a pattern of cornrows braided to the back.

I'm not my hair!

I'M NOT MY HAIR

My hair brings out my confidence!

Even when I cut off my hair for a brand new start,
I still look stunning!

Which celebrity made the popular song
"Whip My Hair"

This is our hair story. How many hairstyles from this book have you rocked before?

Kids HairStory

For more coloring books visit
www.dejhabcoloring.com

Please Follow the brand "Dejha B Coloring" social media pages:

Instagram, TikTok and Facebook pages @DejhaBColoring and tag your coloring pages.
Use Hashtag #DejhaBColoring

Please follow "Black Angel Publishing" social media pages for more Inspirational books

Instagram: @BlackAngelPublishing
Facebook Page: www.facebook.com/BlackAngelPublishing

Test Your Coloring Tools On This Page

Test Your Coloring Tools On This Page

Made in the USA
Middletown, DE
11 March 2022